I0170982

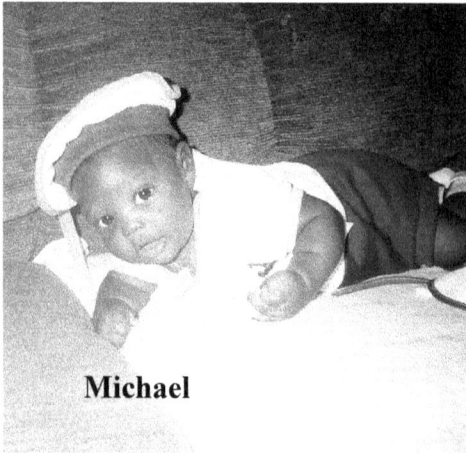

Michael

Mosi

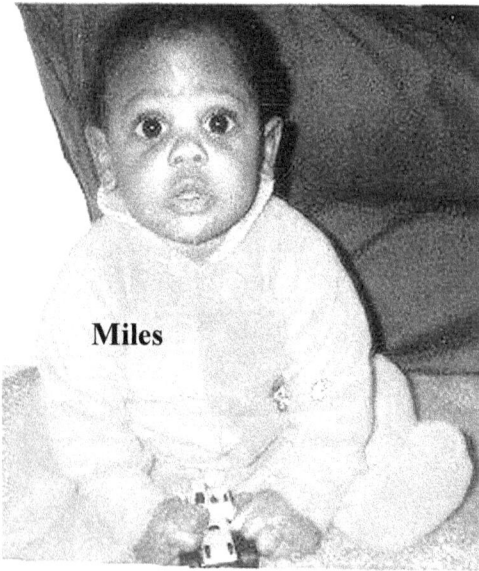

Miles

Michael, Mosi, Miles

Surviving Parenting In The 21st Century:
Have You Seen My Innocence

By
Rufus & Jenny Triplett

Front & Back Cover Design: Rufus & Jenny Triplett
©2015 Dawah International, LLC, a Multimedia Company/
Rufus & Jenny Triplett
Library of Congress Cataloged – In Publication Data
ISBN: **978-0692339114** Dawah International, LLC
Publishing

    Dawah International, LLC Publishing
    PO Box 380
    Powder Springs, GA 30127
    678-389-2646
    dawahinternationalllc@gmail.com

All rights reserved. This book is protected under copyright
laws of the United States of America. No part of this
publication may be reproduced or transmitted in any format
or by any means electronic, mechanical or otherwise,
including photocopying, recording or any other storage or
retrieval system without written permission of the
publisher, except in the case of brief quotations embodied
in critical articles or reviews.
For Worldwide Distribution. Printed in the United States of
America.

FOREWORD

Rufus and Jenny are one of the very few professional husband and wife teams who do just about everything together, while surviving twenty six years of marriage being attached at the hip. Honored as **Ebony Magazine's Couple of the Year in 2012**, and one of the **14 Most Inspiring Black Couples in 2013**, they are known for their motivation, empowerment and healthy examples of happily ever after. Mr. & Mrs. Triplett have traveled extensively and seem to draw attention wherever they appear. With their young look and laid back personalities, they are never far from an intelligent conversation. Their list of accomplishments are long but are highlighted with being military veterans (Marine Corps and Navy respectively) a letter from President Obama, and spotlighted as a **Social Media Power Couple by Mashable.**

Their recent TLC Network special, Rufus and Jenny showcased a small portion of their home life which included their three adult sons, Michael (26), Mosi (24) and Miles (22). Since reflecting on their marriage in their self-published co-authored Amazon Best Seller, *Surviving Marriage In The 21st Century: 13 Easy Tips that Can Help You Get to 20 years and Beyond,* released February 2013 under their own imprint, Dawah International, LLC Publishing, the next questions slanted towards parenting. In this scribe, the Triplett's discuss, in their own humorous way, parenting. They give an overview of how they survived it and can now laugh at it. As not to tell someone else how to raise their children, you will find these anecdotes relatable, comical and better than any metaphor you have ever heard. That tricky little thing called parenting, we are never truly prepared. Rufus and Jenny have some key tips. Below they share one of their favorites.

Here is one of Jenny's Favorites:

- **Parenting…is there an App for that?** – In this technology age we wish we could just download an app and make it all better. Unfortunately we can't. It takes hands on, manual training.

Here is one of Rufus' Favorites:

- **Be there for your kids even if your parents were not there for you** – We still live in a world where too many children are growing up without two parents. Love and support should come from a mother and a father.

DEDICATION

First & foremost we would like to bear witness to the Oneness of God and thank HIM for Blessing us and keeping us together for all of these years and seeing us through the hard times of parenting when we could have easily just washed our hands of our responsibilities. We would also like to thank HIM for keeping us diligent in putting this book together as many have expressed interest in it. May it be of benefit to those that need it.

To our three sons, Michael, Mosi, & Miles. Our lives have been so enriched by you three jointly and severally. You all have grown into some fine young men and may this story be a constant reminder of how we kept you protected. You may not have understood at the time our intentions and your lives may have seemed sheltered, but it was all for the greater good. We always said, "Not on my watch," and we kept that promise. We love you unconditionally. May you instill similar values in your children and keep them protected from the distractions in this world.

To the daughter we never had – your life would have been an inspiration to us just as the boys. Many of the lessons in this book would have been for you. God doesn't give you what you want; he gives you what you need.

Special Words

Please note that we do not condone child abuse or neglect. If anyone is in a relationship where their child is being abused, suspected of being abuse or if you are the abuse, please get help. These tips and stories are to help parents better understand that you are not alone. You are going to go through things that may not be funny at the time, but if you stay strong and keep the faith, you will get through it and be able to laugh about it years later. Abuse and neglect, in any form – mental, verbal, spiritual, sexual and physical, is truly disliked by the both of us.

parenting

[pair-uh n-ting, par-]

noun
1.
the rearing of children:
The schedule allows her very little time for parenting.
2.
the methods, techniques, etc., used or required in the rearing of children:
a course in parenting.
3.
the state of being a parent; parenthood.
adjective
4.
of or concerned with the rearing of children:
good parenting skills.

Surviving Parenting - Be in the Know of New Addictions

Parenting is one of the hardest yet most rewarding jobs you will ever have. You are never quite prepared for it and the task varies for everyone. There is not a one size fits all course and or cure. Being in the know is the first step in helping your preteen/teen navigate through the perils and challenges of puberty and peer pressures.

Among one of the vices that can occur during this wondrous, awkward, curious time for exploring into adulthood, is experimentation. Experimentation can be damaging as it may lead to addictions and even death. Be aware of viral challenges that clog your children's social media streams and tend to be enticing to kids who want to fit in or become popular. Here is a great article from Recovery Corps in regards to the dangers of two of the most popular challenges - drinking hand sanitizer in order to get high and swallowing cinnamon...just because.

Parenting or **child rearing** is the process of promoting and supporting the physical, emotional, social, financial, and intellectual development of a child from infancy to adulthood. Parenting refers to the aspects of raising a child aside from the biological relationship.[1]

The most common caretaker in parenting is the biological parent(s) of the child in question, although others may be an older sibling, a grandparent, a legal guardian, aunt, uncle or other family member, or a family friend.[2] Governments and society may have a role in child-rearing as well. In many cases, orphaned or abandoned children receive parental care from non-parent blood relations. Others may be adopted, raised in foster care, or placed in an orphanage. Parenting skills vary, and a parent with good parenting skills may be referred to as a *good parent*. - **Wikipedia**

INTRODUCTION

This book stemmed from an idea of giving parenting advice to various people after years of being asked "how did you raise three boys to be so mannerable and respectful" or that we have three boys that have all graduated high school, all went to college, no baby daddies and none are in jail. People wanna know…how did we do it? During the course of 2012 & 2013, numerous #SurvivingParenting and #parenting tweets were shared on twitter which helped to create the buzz for this book and we would like to share them with you all in rewind.

Here are several to get you started. Please feel free to share these tips with anyone you think may benefit. Now that does not mean to bootleg the book or take our words as your own…it just means to share what you have learned and how these tips may have been of benefit to you. Also, feel free to read them again and again when you feel as if you have hit a wall and can't go any further. Remember, it's a marathon, not a sprint.

SURVIVING PARENTING TIPS from Twitter

#survivingparenting Parenting is more than a blessing...it's a journey.

#survivingparenting Children are impressionable. They imitate what they see.

#survivingparenting Time sure does fly. Enjoy them while they are young.

#survivingparenting Different shades of us through the years. We evolve as parents.

#survivingparenting Can we look at parenting as a business?

#survivingparenting You know you've survived parenting when you can have dinner with your kids..and they pay

#survivingparenting As an mother of African American boys they turn 25 and are still alive

PARENTING TIPS from Twitter, cont.

#parenting Gasp!!!

#parenting Sigh…where are the parenting controls?

#parenting What life lessons are you teaching your children about money?

#parenting Watch for our parenting segment on Dr. Phil!

#parenting Everybody shouldn't be parents…seriously.

#parenting There are effective ways to discipline your children

#parenting Some things parents do are uncalled for… but I guess you can say that about children too…sheesh

#parenting Group texting with our boys. The 21st Century replacement to "call your mother on Sunday." LOL

#parenting Do you know the latest teen text codes? As a parent…always be aware. Warning…most are pretty sexual.

#parenting Should discipline be for punishment or rehabilitation?

#parenting Parents, what would you do if your child slapped you?

#parenting There are way more single people parenting than there are married people. Different dynamics in the household

#parenting "I didn't know" is no excuse! Pay attention to your kids and their lives!

#parenting I am so tired of these parenting fails. Is there something in the water, the food, the toothpaste, etc.

#parenting What the heck is really going on with people starving kids? How cruel, ignorant, arrogant…

#parenting You can parent from prison

#parenting If only more parents took the time…

#parenting Parenting is not easy

#parenting Strong marriages + strong parents = strong family units

#parenting Parenting, one of the most rewarding things you will ever do in life.

#parenting The ripples of kindness touches many. Teach your children to be kind

#parenting A throwback moment. We took our children on a drive across country

#parenting The more you know, the more you grow in life and as parents

#parenting Parenting can be a circus

#parenting Tough parenting or strict parenting… sometimes its needed

#parenting How to be a great parent in 5 easy steps? Ok.

#parenting Parenting starts at home. Stop letting TV parent your child.

#parenting Good parents are the map that guide children in the right direction

#parenting This is what we used to do to our kids, watch they get us back lol

#parenting Don't be an overbearing mother. Let your child breathe.

#parenting Sometimes spanking is necessary

#parenting Your children will live up to your greatness by watching you live up to yours

#parenting Teach your children culture diversity

#parenting Do you have the right to discipline someone else's child?

#parenting ever compare or compete with other parents

#parenting You can give your children psychological scars by the way you parent

#parenting Parenting takes commitment

#parenting Bad relationships should not ruin a child's life

#parenting …in the words of Tupac "Mama it aint easy trying to raise a man."

#parenting Parenting is not about being your child's friend. You have to be a parent first.

#parenting Never let parenting leave the building

#parenting Giving in to tantrums is opening the door for repeat behavior

#parenting Enjoy the good times, have fun!!!

#parenting This parenting takes a lot of patience… seriously

#parenting Cheering up a child after the loss of a parent takes creativity

#parenting We need to protect our kids from violence and violent message

#parenting We need to protect our kids from prejudices in the media

#**parenting** Parenting is hard!!!

#**parenting** We must build confidence in our children

#**parenting** Are parents responsible for their children's actions…good question

#**parenting** Teenage rebellion is normal. Parents should learn how to deal with it and not stress about it

#**parenting** If Sally jumped off a bridge you think I'm gone let you jump too? Chile puhleeez!!! You don't have Sally's parents…ok.

#**parenting** It's a journey…one you will be happy you started.

#**parenting** a 24/7 job that has no minimum wage and no payday

#**parenting** Hate is a strong word but there are three words that I strongly disliked…what's for dinner?

#**parenting** Who sets a bedtime for 9:45pm?

#**parenting** Social Media monitoring is of the utmost of importance

#**parenting** Take control of explaining sex to your children

#**parenting** hahahahahah sometimes you just gotta laugh

#**parenting** #WWYD

#**parenting** Social media shaming…is that what parenting has become?

#parenting Being a mother is a blessing…but so is being a father

#parenting We believe in family. We believe in parenting.

#parenting The TV was not made to be the babysitter

#parenting The next time you steal, you better steal some knowledge

#parenting It's not something we get to back out of once the choice was made to do it

#parenting Would you leave your children alone for two months and go abroad?

#parenting Parents should know what their kids are texting

#parenting Parenting is an investment. What you put into it is the ROI later on in life

#parenting Parents need to be aware of what's going on in their children's classrooms

#parenting had a ball on Dr Phil show about parenting and decisions

Please note the informal formatting of the tips…hey… it's Twitter…140 characters…okaaay.
Can we get some RT's (retweets… ☺)

✱ ✱ ✱

Our hope for today's children/tweens/teens is to relate to these situations, understand them and make corrections in their lives while there is still time.

Some things in life you live to regret. Some things in life you are blessed to have. And some things in life you overcome and write a story about. These are our stories.

TABLE OF CONTENTS

Am I My Brother's Keeper

It was a sheer blessing to have three boys. In between son #1 and son #2 I suffered a miscarriage. When we talk about it today we say that that was probably our girl. God gives you what you need, not what you want. We welcomed our boys, warmly embraced as knuckleheads, with joy and excitement. Rufus comes from an immediate family of six boys and an extended family of numerous boys. I also have several men in my family as well as a brother that died when I was 6.

With a three bedroom home, the oldest was always slated to get his own room. He was pretty independent, almost from birth, so he grew into his own room and the age of 6. His brothers at the time, 2 & 4, shared a room. But like normal children, the younger boys found themselves wandering into the oldest room. They wanted to play with his things, touch his things, take his things out of his room and into their own. Of course, this became a problem. After several conversations with all three boys and stints of punishments, which included standing on the wall, no play or TV time, the boys just did not want to cooperate. So what did we do…we put them all in the room together. Yup, AM I MY BROTHER'S KEEPER, YES I AM!!!

We had to make a decision to bring more unity and respect with one another so we felt the best way to do that was to make them sleep together, so to speak. We moved the younger two's bunkbeds into the oldest room as it was the larger room and made the other room a play room. So no matter which way you go, you're going to play together, pray together and lay together. This didn't happen until the boys were 7, 9 & 11, but yes, it did happen.

It was touch and go at first. They found new ways to bicker. But after about 8 months and they realized that we were serious and wasn't going to change things back to the way that they were, they started to get along. We were high fiving each other as to the success of our social experiment. We gave constant lectures to them that if something happened to us that it would just be them three and they needed to stick together. Each other is all that they had. A few times they tried to plan against us, what kids don't, but hey found out real quick that we were not the type of parents that they could divide and conquer. Playing mom against dad and dad against mom would be only something they saw on TV or learned from their friends at school. It wasn't happening in our home and not with us.

In reflection, as we did not allow our boys to sleep over every Billy, Bob & Bilals' houses, they had the perfect sleepover, every night. Sometimes we would let them put their sleeping bags on top of their beds like they were having a sleepover. We still have not heard all of the stories they shared and maybe some of the tightest of secrets that they have kept. And maybe we don't want to. What they have between the three of them is a bond that we wanted to be unbreakable. I think we did our job.

Am I My Brother's Keeper Discussion:

Jenny: You know it was something we just had to do.

Rufus: Fo Sho. I was going to do it whether they wanted it or not.

Jenny: Yeah I think unity can definitely be a big part of shaping any childhood.

Rufus: Oh they unified alright. They thought they were going to unify against me. Somebody told them wrong.

Jenny: Yall should have seen the looks on their faces that day we told them what we were going to do

Rufus: What you mean, I did see it. I took a picture. I recorded it for posterity.

Jenny: You did not!!! You should have recorded it. It was a true Kodak moment. You could have copied and pasted it here lol.

Rufus: Its copied and pasted in my long term memory. They probably have it in their short term memories.

Bullying

Bullying has been a part of both of our childhoods. I was bullied for being small and being smart. Rufus was bullied for being a "pretty boy" and being popular with the girls. With this kind of history we knew we had to inform our children of the signs and possibilities of being bullied and how to handle it. Our boys have been in more than a few incidents, more than we can count on one hand, but we will just touch on a few for teaching purposes.

Our oldest son, Michael, was bullied in kindergarten due to ignorance and prejudice. Before he was school age, we moved to a newly built, under construction subdivision. This made him the only Black child in his class and one of very few in the entire school. At lunch one day, a lil boy called him the N word. He in return called him stupid. The other little boy didn't like that so he pushed him. Michael hit him back with a Mike Tyson like blow. Let's just say that blow let everybody know...you don't want none of this. Michael was always a lil heavy handed but a very sweet child. So what happens...we get called to the principal's office for a "conversation." These folks had no idea what they were in for and were truly surprised when the BOTH of us came to the meeting. Oh yes ma'am, two parent household here. So let's talk.

First off, there was already a problem because we were the only parents called in about the situation. Uh...excuse me? Where are the other little racists' parents? Why did the principal try to put it all on our son and say that violence would not be tolerated? I told her, ok, so what are you doing to the little boy that started the whole thing by calling him out of his name? She tried to explain that name calling is not an excuse for hitting someone. I said ok, then what did your staff do when he pushed my child? She was so shocked that I had detailed information about the incident. Why? Because we talk to our children and they talk to us. We express the importance of telling the truth and not making us look like fools when we go to bat for them.

After much roundabout of the situation, the principle assured us that the other little boy would be suspended as well. I don't think that she realized that I would be following up on that. When I found out that nothing happened to the other little boy, the school board was contacted and this situation was further investigated and escalated. The other child was eventually suspended and had to apologize to our son. And the principal had to apologize to us. Moral to the story, don't drop the ball on bullying situations. Most school administrators only see it one way and do nothing about it. Take time to be fluid as a parent. Your kids depend on you.

Another story that stands out is when our two younger sons, Mosi & Miles, detoured a bully by brothering up against him. Our neighbor had some family members staying with her for a length of time and they had a son that enrolled into our boys' school. The neighbor's nephew was a little slow and a little big for his age. Every day he was getting teased and bullied on his way home. (This happened to a little girl in our neighborhood as well; they handled that too) Although our boys walked home they were oblivious to this because they walked in a pack of kids. Our neighbor's nephew would try to run home to beat the crowd leaving him vulnerable to bullies. Once it was brought to our attention, we informed our boys to look for him and start walking him home as he just lived right next door. Welp, one day, it happened. The bully wanted to try all three of them. Mosi & Miles stood their ground against the bully as he tried to single out our neighbor's nephew. Even though both of them were small for their ages, they had strong attitudes and demeanor. So much so, the bully ran off. Needless to say our neighbor's nephew never had another problem When our neighbor found out what had happened, she called in tears. She could not believe that this was all it took to make it stop. We told her that we believed in the old school way of handling things first. Get the children to buddy up and stand up before the parents have to get involved. Most often times kids pick on kids that they think are weak and won't fight back. When they find out that they have people that will stand up for them and with them, it usually goes away. Moral to the story, the village was here. All we had to know was that the problem existed.

With three boys in different grades and numerous extracurricular activities there are so many more stories we could share. The major point is that bullying has existed since and before we were kids. In today's society it's grossly elevated. You have to be on top of it and handle it. Cyber bullying has kids killing themselves. Some of the parents say they did not know. You have to be aware and involved. No one should be able to make your child feel less than or unloved.

Bullying Discussion:

Jenny: See our boys have a little bit of both of us inside of them and I think it comes out at the right times

Rufus: They definitely got a lotta me.

Jenny: That they do. And I'm glad we taught them how to handle certain situations. You don't have to put up with people who think they can tower over you. You don't have to feel powerless. You don't have to be made to feel like you don't belong.

Rufus: All you gotta do is stick together. That's what I taught them. And if somebody hit you, hit them harder. And I bet they will stop.

Jenny: Well you definitely taught them that and a few folks have had to experience what our boys were taught. They just had to tried them for some reason. They soon found out though. That was good instruction.

Rufus: You remember what happened in that lunchroom. My boys did good in that lunchroom.

Jenny: I didn't even talk about that story. They set it off in that lunchroom that day. They set it off.

Rufus: Set it off? They just stood their ground. I created that law before the government made it a law. I told them to handle their business or they would have to come home and deal with me. They didn't want to have to deal with me.

Jenny: Uh..no. You got that right. That they didn't.

Rufus: I didn't want to deal with me.

Chores – Those Doggone Dishes

It's cute when kids want to help around the house at a young age. They imitate cleaning up as it seems fun and feel that they are making a contribution. But when life becomes filled with many other distractions, the work around the house becomes just what they are called... chores. With three children, we felt a sense of comfort that it was going to be easy to keep things clean and kept. There was grass to be cut, vacuuming, laundry, sweeping, mopping, dusting, etc. You name it, there was work to be done. For the most part, we got thru it without micromanaging. But there was one chore that was the gift that kept on giving...a headache. The dishes.

Both of us coming from households with maintained kitchens, the dishes and everything around it was always good to go. Having mothers that could cook and clean the kitchen as she went along so that everything was done by the time you sat down to eat was what we knew. Starting the boys out doing dishes at age 7 on a stool, had already been discussed that it was going to be the norm. Rufus was a chef in the Marine Corps and keeping a tight kitchen a was a must. Little did the boys know...they had some bumpy days ahead.

Introducing them to the easy stuff, cups, glasses, bowls, plates, silverware, etc. and leaving the pots and pans to mom and dad, we thought that would be easy. Washing dishes is not rocket science, but when you don't want to do it, when you want to go play or watch cartoons instead, thus comes the problem. Instead of just doing it right and getting it done so you can be excused, all three of them had to experiment with trying to get over on mom and dad. Hey, they are children. You already know they are going to try you. So why not be prepared for it.

The first time Rufus pulled out a nasty dish, you would have thought that a tsunami was coming and we needed to evacuate. The conversation was had about dirty, nasty dishes, the expectations and another chance was given. All three of them were given chance, after chance after chance. Silverware started to disappear because they didn't want to wash it, plates started to get chipped because of carelessness, a few glasses were broken because of horseplay and the list goes on.

First we tried just giving them their own set of dishes. They had one cup, one bowl, one plate, one fork and one spoon. If they didn't wash their own dishes they were not to touch any other dishes in the kitchen. It worked for a while but laziness set in and they started to sneak other dishes…as if we wouldn't notice. So…we had to try something else. Trial and error. You have to keep trying and never give up on correcting behavior.

At some point, all three were responsible for the kitchen since delegating one week or alternate nights was not working. One person would wash, one person would rinse and check them and one person would check the dried dishes from the night before to make sure nothing was wrong. Welp…that went wrong too. We went old school. The boys were awakened around 2am one morning, had to pull everything out of the cabinets and drawers and rewash. Enough, was enough. After wanting to blame each other for the problem, we let them know that if this continued or if the placing blame on someone else instead of taking responsibility in your part of what's wrong, they would be washing all of the dishes every day.

That cleared things up almost lickity split. No one wanted to continuously wash boatloads of dishes every day when they could be doing something else. Making them responsible for their part as well as not throwing their brother under the bus for something they did was part of the lesson. We gave them breaks at times when we would buy paper plates and plastic ware. Much excitement came when we ate out or ordered in because it meant an easy night. They learned to appreciate the value of hard work. They learned to appreciate the honor in cleanliness. They learned that if they are going to do a job, do it right as there will always be someone checking it. There were many lessons in washing those dishes. We look back on them… and laugh.

Chores – The Dishes Discussion:

Rufus: We showed them that things would get done around here.

Jenny: I don't think I have anything else to say. The story said it all.

Rufus: The story? It was for real. It got real real around here..

Jenny: Yes dear, it was all real. It was probably the most intense chore for sure. Imagine if we had to go thru that with laundry, cutting the grass and everything else.

Rufus: Oh, it was going to get done. It got done.

Jenny: Well fortunately we only had to deal with this with the dishes.

Rufus: We gave them options. What you have to do is give these kids options. I think the biggest thing you need to do is give these kids options. You have the option to do it this way or you have the option to do it this way. They gone figure it out one way or another.

Jenny: It's hard lessons and tough love. But like I said, the story told it all.

Rufus: See, that's what parenting is about. Lots of stories to share.

Driving – Scared to Death

We all know there comes that day in a child's life when they will be interested in getting their leaner's permit, driver's license and learning how to drive. Not necessarily in that order. Since drivers education had been taken out of the schools, parents must put in hours of driving with their child on side roads, main roads, parallel parking and even on the expressway. We started our children out slowly, in parking lots and on streets around our subdivision and other connected subdivisions. The two oldest didn't have it easy because all we had to offer at the time they were learning was a suburban. That was quite a large vehicle for someone just learning how to drive.

Rufus made the decision that he was going to take the lead with Michael. He was the first one to learn and he wanted to teach his son how to drive. It's a man thinking. I totally understood. Michael has never been the most coordinated child so teaching him how to drive without both feet, started out as a challenge. I didn't like being a back seat observer but I had to fall back and let dad do his thing. Well…Michael almost killed us on one occasion and his dad on several others. The rest of the family chose not to ride in the vehicle while he was learning to drive as it was just added pressure and better for me and the other children's safety.

The day came for Michael to take his driving test. We waited a whole year to give him time to learn and be comfortable. He had his own car by then, a Ford Escort. It was smaller and easier to handle. That didn't seem to matter. As I waited for him to return to the DMV with the lady that was giving him the test, as they pulled up, she immediately jumped out of the car and let me know that he almost killed them. Michael was very disappointed. I asked him what happened and he said he just panicked. He said it was like being in the car with daddy. She made him very uncomfortable. No one likes to be in the car with an inexperienced driver and have the feeling that at that moment, it would be all she wrote. What a tough job for those that do it.

At this point, I took over teaching our children. I knew it was going to require patience. The type of patience that a mother could provide. We spent days upon days going over the basics and scoping out the bigger picture. The next time I took him to take his test he passed with flying colors. He had a man riding along this time around and he said he was much more comfortable. He said he asked him a lot of questions about Islam. He said it reminded him of being in the car with me and having casual conversation. He just talked and drove.

Mosi started out learning in the suburban but we eventually went to a minivan. He was much easier to teach because he was a little bit more patient. Almost too patient as he got labeled as the "little old lady" driver of the family. He passed everything on the first try. Miles did as well. It's funny how one child, out of three, can scare the living daylights out of you and the other two have no problems at all. You can't treat all kids the same because they learn differently. Their emotions are different and their motor skills are different.

One thing ya gotta have, or may be two things before getting in the vehicle with these teens. One is patience. The other is guts. And maybe a whole bunch of faith.

Driving Scared to Death Discussion:

Jenny: Boyyy when Mika'il (Michael) started driving, we thought it was going to be a wrap.

Rufus: I didn't.

Jenny: Whaaaat? You were the worst!!! You were the one saying…what you trying to do, kill me?

Rufus: I knew he was going to get it eventually. We took the risk of letting him behind the wheel every time.

Jenny: Well they all got it eventually. And yes lawwwd…it definitely was risky.

Rufus: We all have to be taught.

Jenny: Yup…but it was still an experience.

Rufus: At least we didn't crash. Some people probably crash..

Jenny: True. They probably do. But it was still a terrifying experience.

Cellphones, Social Media & Getting on Our Nerves

When we decided to have children, we had no idea we would be battling something called a flip phone, Myspace or world wide web. It could have been the furthest thing from our minds. Cell phones as we knew them, from back in the 80's, were just pieces of equipment in big ol bags that evolved into huge hand held objects with star wars litesaber like antennas. The late 90's ushered in beepers and even later something of a phone that looked more analog than digital. Discussions of my child never having a beeper turned into discussions about my child never having a cell phone.

Flip phones invaded our "how was school" conversation sometime when the two oldest hit middle school. The boys started seeing other kids with phones and we started having more discussions about why they should or should not have a phone. After much conversation, we decided to go ahead and let them have one so they would not be dinosaurs to technology. But they came with many restrictions. They were not to use them in school unless it was a dire emergency. The only pictures they could take was for contact profiles. The phones were restricted to only two numbers that they could call in middle school, mommy & daddy. When they got to high school it was restricted to mom & a brother or dad and a brother due to the fact that the boys had their own cars and carpooled so meeting up due to extracurricular activities sometimes became an issue. The restrictions came off after homework and housework were done. If there was anything unsatisfactory going on, teachers notes or reports, attitudes around the house, bickering with siblings, bad grades, the phones stayed restricted or disappeared into our room as a punishment. The phones were also subject to search at any time. Text messages, data history, incoming and outgoing phone calls were all checked. This wasn't always on a daily basis but it was done on a routine basis. Oh yes, we paid the bills, we made the rules.

As a reminder, our motto was "not on our watch." You have to know who your kids are talking to and what they are saying and what is being said to them. To many bullies, to many perverts, sexual abuse by trusted individuals, to many people are trying to come after children. Our job was protecting them at all costs. Later for that privacy stuff. You can have privacy when you are old enough to take care of yourself. Ask yourself, how many situations would we hear about with children, the ones that go missing, meeting people on the internet, getting bullied, etc., if we only took more time to be involved as parents?

Being a part of a social network is a privilege, not a right. The phenomenon of Myspace and people connecting from all over the world came into our home like a comet. What a wonderful social experiment and forward way of thinking Even though the idea of it was genius, we thought of so many ways that this could go way wrong. Once again, as not to stifle the boys with the growing technology age, sure, we let them be a part of the online community and use the internet for school purposes. BUT, it came with restrictions as well. The computer was in sight at all times. There were only certain times that they could log in and had to be on and off within a timely manner. No staying on the computer all day and definitely not at unGodly hours. Even on a weekend, if you hadn't brushed your teeth yet, made your bed, made your prayers, or ate breakfast, you couldn't just hop on the computer.

Having the computer screen in full view stops a lot of sneaky behavior. Knowing that someone is looking over your shoulder you are less likely to do doubtful things. We were privy to all passwords and anything obscene that came across the screen from other people's profiles, they had to go. Delete, delete, delete. Being responsible for what our children ingest is a part of parenting. Part of our jobs is to block out what does not need to be seen in adolescence and a lot of times some of that stuff doesn't need to be seen in a adulthood either. That's part of the innocence. Have you seen my innocence? When speaking about our children, we should be able to answer yes.

Not only did cell phone monitoring, internet monitoring and social media monitoring get on our nerves, but we knew it was something we had to do. We don't have to shelter our kids from everything, we can allow them to participate, within parameters. And now that our boys are in the millennial stage and look back on it all, we think they agree. How do we know…they tend to laugh about these stories just as much as we do.

Cellphones & Social Media Discussion

Rufus: Social Media headache my foot.

Jenny: You know we had 99 problems with those boys and social media, cell phones and the internet all seemed to be wrapped up into one.

Rufus: Yeah, they had problems, but I was the problem solver.

Jenny: I think by saying that we did it this way for their own good, people may look at it as a little strict or invasive.

Rufus: Call it what you want. It's too many child…what they call em…

Jenny: Molesters

Rufus: No

Jenny: Abusers

Rufus: No. Child abductions and that wasn't about to happen on my watch. They could like it or not like it. It wasn't happening over here captain.

Jenny: I'm sure they will pull form these stories and use some of this with their children because their kids are going to be on a whole nother level.

Rufus: They already been pulling from a lot of stuff that we have taught them. And yeah…kids are off the chain these days.

Jenny: Raising kids and having to go through what we went thru was a good lesson for us.

Rufus: Hmph. It was a good lesson for them. It's called parenting.

Well…there ya have it. A few of the stories throughout our parenting journey. May it be of benefit to you. There are no perfect parents. It's on the job training. If you stay alert and stay vested, you just might come out of this thing with minimal scratches. First aid is always available. But what you can't fix with a band-aid, you can fix with apple pie… maybe (smiles) This is Jenny from the block and I'm dropping the mic.

EMPTYNESTERS TIPS for the Road…

Oh you will…eat out often #emptynesters

Dropping off and picking up the kids at college campuses #emptynesters

Home alone…and loving it #emptynesters

Coffee became a new friend #emptynesters

Playing Xbox and watching TV Shows uninterrupted #emptynesters

Sitting here getting ready to write and had a thought of wonder what our boys are doing…it passed lol. #emptynesters

Very spoiled having an empty nest. Love to see the boys come, love to see them go. #emptynesters

Grown kids moving back home? For the love of goodness why…but it happens. #emptynesters

The boys are turning a year older, guess that's how we'll start counting being without kids lol #emptynesters

Need me a car. Maybe a sports car. Maybe a Camaro or Corvette. Midlife crisis? Nah an empty nest makes you empowered. Yes!!! #emptynesters

Never a dull moment in our household but we do love the quiet times of our empty nest #emptynesters

Can't wait to get our house back! #emptynesters

Cherish the moments, they do grow up fast. #emptynesters

Enjoying freedom! #emptynesters

Big kids at heart #emptynesters

Those three words…what's for dinner? Even as emptynesters they are like fingernails on a chalkboard. Hubby hush!!! #emptynesters

Reflecting…we've raised three great men #emptynesters

Even though we are empty nesters it seems like the work is never done. #emptynesters

Sometimes you thing you will never make it to an empty nest #emptynesters

Empty Nesters need to be organized. #emptynesters

Our Motto – Not on Our Watch. We kept our boys safe and protected. #emptynesters

Internet access was only allowed I plain sight. Passwords were a must. No obscene profiles. Worked wonders. #emptynesters

An empty nest is full of opportunities. #emptynesters

We stayed old school. God gave us three baby daddies with knuckleheads and no scrubs lol. #emptynesters

Create classics for future generations. #emptynesters

Headed to Niagara Falls. No kids to worry about. Beautiful. #emptynesters

We never turn off parenting. We just provide care in stages. #emptynesters

Tripism - Two fun-loving people will always find the "fun" in everything they do. #emptynesters

✳ ✳ ✳

Three Tips on How to Parent in the Digital Age avoiding Pimps, Players and the Prison Pipeline

Technology is ever evolving and of all of the generations that seems to be gadget geeks and in tune with everything social is the teeny boppers of the now generation. Facebook, Twitter, Instagram and Foursquare, entertains traffic from teens from all over the world. Smart phones, laptops and netbooks have become a parents' worst nightmare.

Rufus and Jenny Triplett are motivational speakers that tour and speak to middle and high schools, DRUG COURTS, juvenile facilities, group homes, families in crisis, and non-profit organizations alike about the teen experience and the importance of making better decisions. Parents are invited to these presentations as tips are given on how to have less confusion in the home and get through the teen aged years without murdering their children.

Parenting will not be the same in a single parent household versus a two-parent household. Proper monitoring can be done in any household if the rules are set and monitored. Parents should never have any excuses as to ensuring the well-being of their children. These three basic how to's could save a family from unnecessary headaches and heartaches:

- Parents should monitor computer access. Computers should be in a central location in the home where the screen can be visible at all times. Privacy is a privilege and not a right.

- Parents should have all passwords to social and email accounts. There should never be a time when a parent does not know that their child is sexting, being cyberbullied, doing drugs or being sexually active. Sporadic checks of accounts are warranted.

- Parents should monitor relationships with family members, friends, and casual contacts (i.e. coaches, teachers, tutors, babysitters, etc.) Most often times inappropriate relationship comes from trusted individuals.

Child molesters, prostitution rings, and sugar daddies are around every corner. A less than aggressive style of parenting allows these predators to gather their victims easily. Parents are for guidance and protection. The best way to accomplish either is communication. Establishing rules are not always an easy task, but if the rules come with understanding, the lessons might not be learned the hard way.

✳✳✳

ABOUT THE CO-AUTHORS

Rufus and Jenny are one of the very few professional husband and wife teams who do just about everything together, while surviving over twenty five years of marriage being attached at the hip. Honored as **Ebony Magazine's Couple of the Year in 2012**, and one of the **14 Most Inspiring Black Couples in 2013**, they are known for their motivation, empowerment and healthy examples of happily ever after. Mr. & Mrs. Triplett have traveled extensively and seem to draw attention wherever they appear. With their young look and laid back personalities, they are never far from an intelligent conversation. Their list of accomplishments are long but are highlighted with being military veterans (Marine Corps and Navy respectively) a letter from President Obama, and spotlighted as a **Social Media Power Couple by Mashable.**

Rufus Triplett, Jr., originally from Flint, Michigan and a1986 graduate of Flint Northern High School, is a talented singer, songwriter and producer. He co-wrote, produced and toured for the platinum group Ready for the World in the late 80's. He chose to broaden his horizons in the Marine Corps where he went to school for Culinary Arts. After relocating to Atlanta in the early 90's he found a love for computers and has become a technology geek. Not only can he build them from scratch but he has become the "go to" guy for all of his family members. His parents, Rufus Triplett, Sr., a retired firefighter for the City of Flint, and Donzella Triplett, a school teacher for Flint Public Schools, have resided in Flint for over 40 years.

Jenny Triplett, originally from Saginaw, Michigan and a 1986 graduate of Arthur Hill High School, always aspired for a career in media. Starting out as an intern at a 107 FM under DJ Dave Rosas, she established a relationship with several entertainers and Ready for the World where she went on to head their marketing outreach team. Jenny also chose to explore the military where she gained a wealth of knowledge and experience during her time in the United States Navy. After marrying Rufus and relocating to Atlanta she headed her own entertainment company for over 14 years which included concert promotions and the children's group Kidsworld. Their flourishing company was halted during the time Jenny dealt with legal issue and a brief period of incarceration. The Triplett's do not consider that ta dark period in their lives because their marriage grew stronger and they bonded to the point where their relationship became unshakeable. Her parents, Eugene and Mary Jennings are deceased.

The Triplett's co-own Dawah International, LLC, a multimedia company, which published Prisonworld Magazine for eight years, co-hosts of their own weekly radio show, the Prisonworld Radio Hour which airs in podcast and is syndicated to iTunes and tunein. They also have two successful blogs and are requested keynote and session speakers and for various platforms which include corporations, wellness retreats, correctional facilities, non-profit organizations, schools, radio shows and print magazines.

Recently airing in a TLC Network special, Rufus and Jenny are celebrated for their rewarding and highly requested marriage workshops that keeps them on the road several weeks out of the year. Their exciting couples travel adventures have benefited in sponsorships and spawned workshops for singles seeking marriage as well. Now adding self-published co-authors and Amazon Best Sellers to their long list of accomplishments, ***Surviving Marriage In The 21st Century: 13 Easy Tips that Can Help You Get to 20 years and Beyond,*** released February 2013 under their own imprint, Dawah International, LLC Publishing, is sparking the much needed conversation about marriage and that tips needed to survive the foundation and institution of the family that it has always been.

Always adding to their media personalities rcsume, appearing in magazines such as Redbook, Ladies Home Journal and Black Enterprise helped them to crossover to live television. They were credentialed as Marriage Experts by Huff Post Live as well as frequently invited guests that always provides a marriage message that resonates with humor and reality. Their appearances on Family Court with Judge Penny and Dr. Phil garnered rave reviews as to their parenting philosophies which is explored in this release – ***Surviving Parenting in the 21ˢᵗ Century – Have You Seen My Innocence***. Jenny's appearance on The Mike & Juliet Morning show was phenomenal as she gave The Real Housewives of Atlanta a little wisdom. Jenny is a featured blogger for the Huffington Post and has provided comments for CNN, Black Enterprise Magazine, Ebony Magazine, MSN.com, The LA Times, The American Prospect Magazine, Google News, Brides.com, Lagos Times (Nigeria), Reuters, and a host of other magazine and radio shows.

Being parents of three boys, Michael, 26, Mosi, 24 and Miles 22, they know the trial and tribulations of not only raising children, but African-American men who could end up as stereotypes. They are passionate about family and detouring young men and women from the criminal justice system. Some of the subjects they speak about are dysfunctional families, substance abuse, entrepreneurship, marriage & relationships, self-conscious addictions, incarceration, stereotypes and the list goes on.

Anyone dealing with inmates has to have a tough demeanor. The Triplett's like to take the non-judgmental and forgiveness approach with their work. Dealing with educating inmates and their families brings great satisfaction to the couple knowing they are a part of improving someone's life.

CONTACT
Rufus & Jenny Triplett
678-233-8286
www.rufusandjennytriplett.com

Military Babies

Giving birth in a military hospital on a military base is a unique experience. Being pregnant while in the military is different as well. If you are on active duty, you receive a consultation about prenatal care as soon as your command is notified of your pregnancy. Medical appointments are mandatory and they do not hesitate to put you on report if you do not go or put you on light duty if there is anything sketchy about your pregnancy.

Our oldest son was born while I was on active duty and stationed in Norfolk, VA. The maternity ward at that hospital was very, very old. It felt surreal and like something out of One Who Flew Over the Cuckoo's Nest. There were old iron beds, quilted blankets, robes and slippers that looked like they were from the 60's and a recovery room that was the size of a closet.

After a very grueling C-section, they let you rest. Since I knew I had to get up and take care of my baby, I chose not to rest. I got up and moved around as much as possible. Other ladies in the ward couldn't believe it. They were saying they stayed sedated for days. I told them that my mother would have a fit knowing that I had a baby that depended on me and I'm just lying in the bed.

The nurses would not bring my son to me until I had a conniption. They told me that with C-section patients the baby was not allowed to stay with the mother until after three days. I told them that was not going to work and that they better bring my baby before I talked to someone in charge and filed a complaint..

Mosi was born at the hospital on Andrews Air Force Base. His doctor was awesome. I labored long, very long, on my birthday. It was a difficult all-natural birth. In addition to having a bowel movement inside of me during labor, they could not stabilize his heartbeat. In just a few hours of his birth he was medevacked out to John Hopkins hospital because of his irregular heartbeat. They brought him back within 24 hours and let me see him immediately. It was a nerve racking time. Just when I thought I was going home in a timely manner, I was hit with an infection and a fever that would not go away. It kept me in the hospital for a week and I still went home without my baby. The military takes every extra precaution so he had to stay a few extra days after I left.

With everything that happened with the first two kids, Miles birth seems uneventful. The normal back and forth to the hospital because of false labor and the slow to dilate played a part, but not being able to get the care at a military hospital because it was too far away worried us a bit. The most abnormal things that happened was that the doctor almost missed the birth. She showed up only after I was already pushing, and when he was born, he didn't cry. Not a sound. He didn't say a word until the nurses started messing with him. I thought my baby was dead. Nope, he was just laid back and very quiet. And he's still that way today.

Military marriages experience more than their share of obstacles. The most unbearing at times is the mandatory deployment for tours of duties which requires the service member to leave spouse and children behind. The separation can go very well or very wrong. It can lead to a deepening strength of affection or it can lead to acts of infidelity. Fortunately and unfortunately we have witnessed both. Fortunately and unfortunately we have seen the survival and demise of both. It is very possible for two people jump in the foxhole together and fight for happily ever after. We were fortunate as we never had to experience a deployment due to Rufus' position as a chef for the officers which included the Commandant of the Marine Corps. Our separation due to military orders was limited to field maneuvers and drills and a three week duty station. You could say that I was feeling like the wife of Steven Segal. We were young and in love and we survived. We were thankful for so much support from so many serving that we knew it was possible. To all who are surviving a marriage and raising kids involving the military in some shape, form or fashion, WE salute you.

✳ ✳ ✳

ACKNOWLEDGEMENTS

Sending special shout outs and thanks to our children Michael, Mosi & Miles Triplett (very affectionately known as our three grown knuckleheads), our parents, Rufus Sr. & Donzella Triplett, still married and together after 46 years, (Jenny's parents are both deceased), Grandma Triplett (who is 95 years young) our siblings, our 23 nieces and nephews and a number of very special friends who have been huge supporters and encouragement along the way. We will not name you all personally because if we forget someone we are sure to be slammed on Facebook and/or Twitter or Instagram and only celebrities "beef" on social media. So with that said…yall know who you are.

To all of the publishers, freelance writers, magazine staff and publicists who have given input and guidance along the way. Your value and support is most appreciated. To the staff at Dr Phil, Ebony Magazine, the Huffington Post and Huff Post Live, thanks so much. Yall rock!

From Allah we came and to Him we shall return…

Parenting Experts are Concerned with The Class of 2011 Legacy: Cyberbullying, Sexting and Teen Pregnancy Pacts

High school is one of the most anticipated times for a teen. It is a time where you live care free, hang out with friends, and come to discover your path in life. That is what the majority of teens actually experience. There is another side a high school life, a dark side of high school, where teens experience some of the most unpleasant and unmentionable situations that scar them mentally for the rest of their lives.

Prisonworld LIVE, a motivational speaking tour that speaks to middle and high schools, DRUG COURTS, juvenile facilities, group homes, families in crisis, and non-profit organizations alike about the teen experience and the importance of making better decisions. "As adults, we have all had the teen experience. My high school experience was good and bad. I shared that with my three boys 17, 19 and 21 in hopes to make their experiences the best possible. I did not give in to peer pressure like smoking and drinking, but I was bullied. I had to make hard choices to stay away from people who called themselves my friends. Being a cheerleader made me popular. Being smart made me disliked. Being small made me a target. Who better to give advice than someone who has endured it all? Once I tell my story and how I got through it, it really inspires the kids to keep their heads up." says Jenny Triplett, co-producer of Prisonworld LIVE.

Natasha MacBryde, a 15 year old who committed suicide by walking in front of a train after a relentless campaign of cyberbullying, is just one of numerous teens who are succumbing to the torture that teens are enduring on a daily basis. In the new age of technology, kids are finding ways to push buttons of those who are just trying to live their lives and exist on a daily basis.

Sex drugs and rock-n-roll was a phrase that defined a generation. Sexting will now be a defining term of teens in the new millennium. Exposing your body parts to the opposite sex, or even the same sex, is a new phenomenon that has rejuvenated and brought satisfaction to raging hormones. Reports of unwanted sexual advances have increased as well reports of teens actually having sex in class and those who have made pregnancy pacts.

"I come from a home with six boys. Our hormones were off the chain but these teens have taken things to a whole new level. We never exposed ourselves in any way to girls and they may have wanted to be touched but we did that with caution. It just seems that these teens are so wild and free and are just letting it all hang out. They are worse than the seventies, eighties and nineties put together. I remember when coming to school pregnant use to be an embarrassment. When the school found out, you would have to leave and go to a special school. Now it's so common that some schools come with daycares. Facebook, Twitter, YouTube and all of these other social networks needs better monitoring by parents. Parents have a responsibility to guide and protect. As adults, we have to start the conversation, open the conversation, and keep the conversation going. That is what we did with our three boys and I am proud to say that I have no "baby daddies" for sons." says Rufus Triplett, co-producer of Prisonworld LIVE.

In 2008, teens took to YOUTUBE to rally other teens to get involved with a pregnancy pact. Eight teens in Boston made national news by becoming pregnant at the same time. Their high profile coverage resulted in appearances on several national talk shows and eventually spawned the show Teen Mom on MTV. The conversation was started and opened to teens to express their feelings as to prevent another such happening. In 2010, another pregnancy pact made national news when seven teenage girls decided to get pregnant all at the same time. The work is far from over. Prisonworld LIVE continues the conversation.

The Confession of a Teenage Mother

The Final Exam

Now I can look back and analyze some of the things that went wrong in my life. The most painful part is realizing that I, too, had a hand in my own failures. Sure, my parents and teachers can take part of the blame, but there is still enough left for me.

Take, for example, the situation surrounding my menstrual cycle. I was 13 years old when I had my first period, and I don't know what was happening to me. My mother never kept up with that. I am a grown married woman today and even my husband keeps up with such matters. I felt that she didn't care and left that situation up to me to take care of. After all, that was what she did when I was pregnant.

Then there was the Family Planning or Birth Control Clinic that I walked in and out of with my friends. There were people on that staff who would have been very willing to counsel me about protected sex. I knew this, but I didn't act on it. Instead, I ran to friends who didn't know much more than I did. I could have talked to Mrs. Ressman or my sister-in-law early on, instead of waiting until it was too late. So many things could have changed my entire life if only I had taken advantage of them. But that's all behind me now. My teenage years are long since gone. If you are a teenager reading this book, you still have a chance to take control of your life by getting the information you need to help you grow into an intelligent, productive, and well-adjusted person.

Never deny your feelings about sex. Talk to someone whom you trust. That person can be more objective in helping you to avoid making a mistake. And, what's more important, he or she won't laugh at you or belittle what you are thinking or feeling. That person cares about you and will want the best for you. If you don't have a close friend or mentor, then go to a counselor or health professional. Whether they care about you or not, they can at least give you accurate information about sexual intercourse and it's consequences. And there's no stigma attached to asking questions.

Let's take a simple question - one that I should have asked the counselors at Planned Parenthood. Why use a condom? It's simple - the odds of not getting pregnant or contracting a disease are greater if you use one; that's basic information. The only thing these counselors can't or won't tell you is that a condom won't protect you from the loss of your self-respect or a guilty conscience, especially if you have been taught not to do such things until you are married.

Let's take another issue, like males. Young men are interesting creatures. They don't necessarily think like we do. Contrary to what most young girls believe, guys won't hate you if you don't give in to their desires. The may be temporarily upset that they couldn't get their way, but they will still like you - that is, if they liked you in the first place. Get over the fact that if you don't give them sex, someone else will. At that age, sex shouldn't be you main concern. Many young men will have sex with whoever is willing and offering. Does the fact that they can get sex somewhere else alter your life? The sexual experience means very little to a young male. Some may consider it a graduation from boyhood to manhood. Some may do it because of peer pressure. And then there might be that one young man who is truly in love. Still, the act seldom involves lasting feelings like love.

Young girls are often a lot faster at making commitments than boys. That's just the way it is. We just want to make him ours. Then we can start telling him he cannot look at other girls. You should not have to make demands like that to have a relationship. One of the differences between boys and men, other than biology, is a sense of responsibility and commitment. If he loves you, he'll make the commitment on his own. Like every other attribute, responsibility and commitment must grow and develop gradually - and it should. It cannot happen overnight; it takes time and maturity. Don't try to force it on a teenager.

Teen years are experimental years. Drugs, drinking, reckless driving, and sex are just a few of the experiments. But most teens are not ready to face the consequences of their actions. They are not equipped with the knowledge or emotions needed for adult behaviors. These attributes will develop when you actually become an adult. As teenagers, you will go through many stages before you reach adulthood.

Some of you are anxious to know the game of life and how you play it. You want to be street smart and experience the real world. I know because I wanted to. Let me take this opportunity to tell you I wish I would have been book smart too. The combination would have served me much better as an adult. Most of us have career goals and dreams we want to fulfill. Believe me, if you have an education, those career goals and dreams are far more reachable. Education gives us access to society in a respectable, acceptable way. Street smarts rely on trickery and deception. Once we are discovered using those means to live, we are criticized by the larger masses and no longer have access to the good life we all seek. We prepare for just thirteen years for the real world. The rest of life is just the final exam.

www.ingramcontent.com/pod-product-compliance
Lightning Source LLC
Chambersburg PA
CBHW060719030426
42337CB00017B/2919